MOUNT EVEREST
THE HIGHEST MOUNTAIN

Aileen Weintraub

The Rosen Publishing Group's
PowerKids Press™
New York

Published in 2001 by The Rosen Publishing Group, Inc.
29 East 21st Street, New York, NY 10010

First Edition

Book Design: Michael de Guzman, Emily Muschinske
Layout: Kim Sonsky

Photo Credits: Background Image on all pp. and p. 4 © Craig Lovell/CORBIS; p.7 © CORBIS; p. 8 © Hulton-Dutsch Collection/CORBIS; p. 11 © Shedan Collins/CORBIS; p. 12, 15, 16 © Galen Rowell/CORBIS; p. 14 © Keren Su/ CORBIS; p.19 © Bettmann/CORBIS; p.20 © CORBIS.

Weintraub, Aileen, 1973–
    Mount Everest : the highest mountain / Aileen Weintraub.—1st ed.
      p. cm.— (Great record breakers in nature)
    ISBN 0-8239-5636-9 (alk. paper)
    1. Mountaineering—Everest, Mount (China and Nepal)—History—Juvenile literature. 2. Everest, Mount (China and Nepal)—Description and travel—Juvenile literature. [1. Everest, Mount (China and Nepal) 2. Mountaineering.]
I. Title. II. Series.

GV199.44.E85 W45 2000
796.52'2'095496—dc21   00-036712

Manufactured in the United States of America

CONTENTS

4

HIGH IN THE SKY

What would it be like if you could touch the sky? If you were standing at the top of Mount Everest, you might know what that feels like. Mount Everest is the highest mountain **peak** in the world. At 29,028 feet (8,848 m) high, Mount Everest is almost five and a half miles (9 km) high! Mount Everest is one of the many peaks that make up the Himalaya Mountains. The Himalayan mountain range runs through the countries of Tibet and Nepal on the **continent** of Asia. Mount Everest is so big that half of it is in Nepal and half of it is in Tibet.

◄ *Mount Everest is part of the Himalayan mountain range. The name Himalaya means "home of snow."*

THE HIGHEST PEAK

Mount Everest wasn't always the highest mountain. Millions of years ago earthquakes in that **region** caused Earth's crust to crumble. The earthquakes forced land that was underwater to push upward. The land reached higher and higher until it formed the highest peak in the world. No one knew exactly how tall Mount Everest was until 1841. That was when Sir George Everest, the British **surveyor** general of India, recorded the location and height of the mountain. There was so much excitement about Sir George's discovery that years later the mountain was named after him. Mount Everest became known as "the roof of the world."

Many scientists and photographers study Mount Everest. ▶

THE DANGER ZONE

In 1924, two British men named George Mallory and Andrew Irvine were willing to risk death to be the first to climb Everest. They disappeared on the mountain, and no one ever saw them alive again. In 1999, an **expedition** tried to discover what had happened to the two men. Only Mallory's body was found. It was buried in the snow high up on the mountain.

On May 29, 1953, Sir Edmund Hillary and a **Sherpa** named Tenzing Norgay had better luck. They were the first to climb to the highest point on Earth. Using ladders, ropes, and axes to help them climb, they finally reached the top of Mount Everest.

◀ *Hillary and Norgay could only stay at the top of Mount Everest for 15 minutes. After that they would have run out of oxygen.*

THE SHERPAS

Climbing Mount Everest is very difficult. Without the Sherpas, many people could not safely climb the mountain. Sherpas find Mount Everest easier to climb than people who don't live in the mountain region. This is because they have **adapted** to their environment. They are used to the cold air and high **altitudes.** With the help of the Sherpas, explorers have been able to map out routes on Mount Everest. The Sherpas also help mountain climbers by carrying about 45 pounds (20.4 kg) of food and supplies up the mountain. Climbers can take several months to reach the top of Mount Everest.

This is a picture of Sherpa children. The Sherpas call Mount Everest Chomolungma, meaning "goddess mother of the world." ▶

WHAT'S THE WEATHER LIKE UP THERE?

The very top of Mount Everest is called the **summit**. The top of Mount Everest is one of the coldest places on Earth. In the summer, the temperature at the summit can be as cold as -40 degrees Fahrenheit (-40° C). There is snow and ice on the mountain all year round.

Winds at the summit can reach speeds of 130 miles (209.2 km) an hour. On Mount Everest, storms called **monsoons** happen when there is a lot of wind and rain. Sometimes the rain turns to hard ice and can be very harmful. The winds are so strong on the summit during a monsoon that they can knock a person right over.

◄ *Climbers need special equipment to protect themselves from the cold at the top of Mount Everest. This climber has a tent, boots, and warm clothing.*

LIFE ON MOUNT EVEREST

People don't live on Mount Everest. As you climb higher, the air becomes thinner. This means that there is less oxygen in the air. The air is also very cold. Climbers have to wear **oxygen** tanks to help them get enough air to breathe.

Animals called yaks help climbers carry equipment part of the way up the mountain. Yaks have thick coats. Their coats help them adjust to the mountain air. Yaks are strong and can safely climb icy slopes. Other animals that live on the mountain are sheep, tigers, goats, leopards, and many kinds of birds and insects.

This picture shows yaks climbing Mount Everest. An insect called the jumping spider also lives on the mountain. This spider can live on Everest at a height of up to 22,000 feet (6,706 m). ▶

PLANTS ON THE HIGHEST MOUNTAIN

The foot of Mount Everest is rich in plants and trees. You can find birch trees, juniper trees, blue pines, and **rhododendrons**. Plants grow better on the eastern part of the mountain because there is more rainfall on that side. Mountain climbers see fewer and fewer plants as they get closer to the summit. This is because the air is too thin and too cold high up on the mountain for anything to live and grow. As climbers go higher, they will see only shrubs. Soon the shrubs disappear, too. By the time a climber reaches the summit, there are just blankets of white snow for miles (km) around.

Plants like the rhododendrons shown here grow at the foot of Mount Everest. As climbers head toward the summit, they will see only shrubs.

MYTHS AND MONSTERS ON EVEREST

For a long time, little was known about the highest mountain in the world. People made up stories and myths about Mount Everest. The Sherpas once believed that there were four-toed monsters with pointy heads who lived deep in the mountain's snow. They called these monsters Yetis. They believed that these monsters were half man, half ape. Other people called these monsters **abominable snowmen**. Some still believe that religious spirits or ghosts live on the mountain. Many of the people who live nearby think that Mount Everest is **sacred** because it is the highest place on Earth.

Some people believe that the footprint in this photo belongs to an abominable snowman. ▶

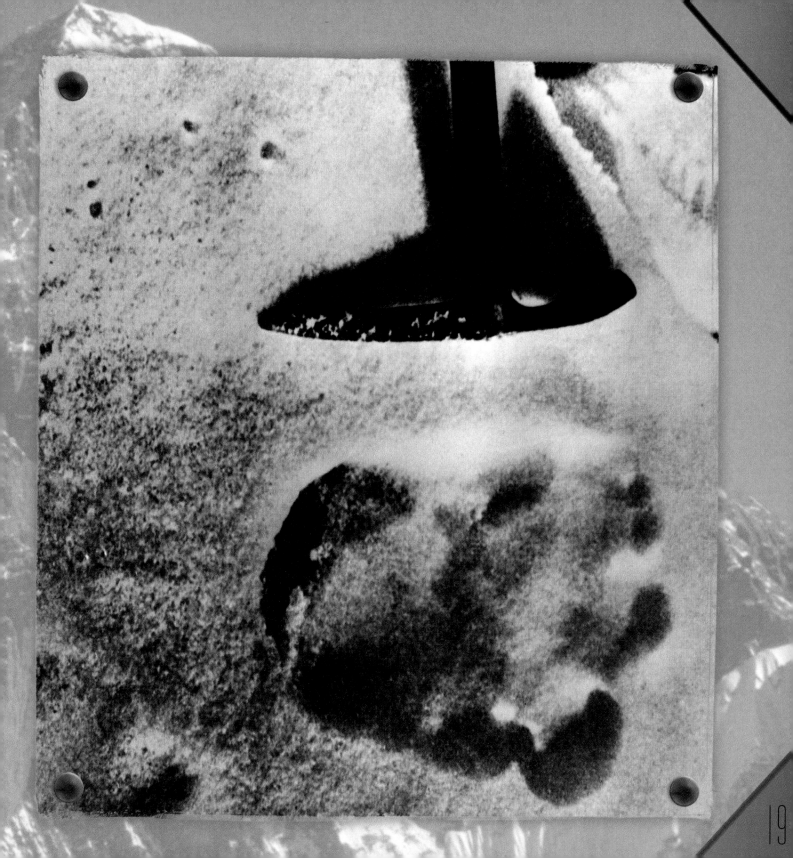

19

DANGER! DANGER!

Since 1924, over 4,000 people have tried to climb Mount Everest. Only 660 people have reached the summit. One hundred and forty-two have died trying. Others have turned back because of the cold, thin air, high winds, and bad weather. Moving **glaciers** are another reason that people have turned back. Changes in the weather can cause glaciers to start moving. As the glaciers move, loose snow can roll down the mountain causing an **avalanche**. Avalanches on Everest can go up to 72 miles (116 km) per hour. If a person does not get out of the way in time, he or she could be crushed by the ice and snow.

◄ This is an avalanche on Mount Everest. Avalanches on the mountain can move as fast as 72 miles (116 km) per hour.

REACHING NEW HEIGHTS

Climbers need a lot of equipment to make the dangerous journey up Mount Everest. Today climbers carry at least 30 pounds (13.6 kg) of equipment with them. This includes climbing ropes, sleeping bags, tents, small stoves, and oxygen tanks. They also bring a lot of food, including pasta, canned fish, and even candy.

Climbing to the top of Mount Everest takes a great amount of effort. Climbers have to prepare for a long time to meet this challenge. They need to be in good physical shape before attempting to climb the highest mountain. These brave climbers risk their lives to touch the sky and see "the roof of the world"!

GLOSSARY

abominable snowmen (ah-BOM-en-ahbl SNOH-men) Mysterious creatures that some people think live in the Himalayas.

adapted (uh-DAPT-ed) Changed to fit certain conditions.

altitudes (AL-tih-toodz) Heights above Earth's surface.

avalanche (AHV-uh-lanch) A large amount of snow sliding down a mountain.

continent (KON-tin-ent) One of seven great masses of land on Earth.

expedition (ek-spuh-DIH-shun) A trip for a special purpose, such as a scientific study.

glaciers (GLAY-shurz) Large masses of ice that move down a mountain.

monsoons (mohn-SOONZ) Types of weather made up of strong winds and rain.

oxygen (AHK-sih-jin) A gas in air that has no color, taste, or odor, and is necessary for people and animals to breathe.

peak (PEEK) The very top of the mountain, ending in a point.

region (REE-jen) A part of Earth.

rhododendrons (row-duh-DEN-drenz) Trees or shrubs with pink, white, or purple flowers.

sacred (SAY-kred) Highly respected and considered very important.

Sherpa (SHERP-ah) A person from Tibet who lives in the Nepal region of the Himalayas.

summit (SUM-it) The highest part of a mountain, where the peak is.

surveyor (ser-VAY-er) Someone who measures land.

INDEX

WEB SITES

To learn more about Mount Everest, check out these Web sites:

http://www.mteverest.com

http://www.everestnews.com